Contents

1 What is bullying?

Bullying is an ugly word and an ugly activity. For the person who is bullied, the experience is one of pain, fear, **humiliation** and often despair. Bullying takes many different forms and is carried out by all kinds of people.

Hurtful behaviour

Bullying is any activity that is done deliberately to hurt someone or make him or her feel bad. It usually builds up, becoming a sequence of cruel or **intimidating** behaviour. Bullying may be direct or indirect.

Direct bullying may take the form of repeated physical violence such as persistent hitting, pulling hair, burning with cigarettes, cutting, bending fingers back and so on. Sometimes threats of violence are not followed through, but they leave the target living in fear. Direct bullying also includes stealing or destroying someone's belongings, verbal abuse and **cyber-bullying** – using technology to **harass** someone (see pages 18–23).

Physical bullying ranges from pushing and punching someone to causing serious injury.

Taking or damaging someone's possessions are common types of bullying.

'Bullying is a problem that large numbers of kids confront on a daily basis at school; it's not just an issue for the few unfortunate ones.'

Jaana Juvonen, Professor of Psychology, University of California in Los Angeles, USA

Indirect bulling typically involves getting at someone through other people. It may mean spreading rumours, turning someone's friends against him or her, isolating someone by not involving him or her in conversations and social activities, or getting someone into trouble.

Speaking out

People may be bullied as small children, teenagers or even adults. Bullying can have terrible and often lasting **psychological** effects on the target – and also on the bully.

It can be very difficult to tell anyone if you are being bullied, as it seems shameful. It's easy to think there is something wrong with you that is causing the bullying – but that's exactly what the bullies want you to think. Bullying can happen to anyone, and everyone has the right to stop it.

IT HAPPENED TO ME

A group of kids used to get at me because they thought my clothes looked cheap and they had flashy stuff. At school, they could only say things, but on the way home they used to throw stones at me. I tried to ignore them, but it got worse. Once, one of them threatened me with a knife, and another waved a cigarette lighter over my clothes saying they would set light to my stupid outfit. That was when I told my class teacher, and soon it was sorted out. She spoke to them, and sent letters to their parents, and they were told to stay away from me.

Agnes, 15

'There are standard short, medium and long term impacts of bullying that we see over and over again and they would include really poor self-esteem, mood disorders, anxiety disorders, self-harm, eating disorders and in very rare cases, suicide.'

Dr Michael Carr-Gregg, Child Psychologist, Melbourne, Australia

A young person may be vulnerable to bullies on the journey to and from school, including on the school bus or at the bus stop.

Any time, any place

Bullying can happen anywhere, but it is most common at times and places where the target is easily isolated and **vulnerable**, and away from people who are likely to **intervene**. It's often somewhere the target has to go, so he or she can't avoid the bullies. Many young people are bullied on school premises – in corridors or staircases, in the changing rooms or toilets, in the playground, sports fields or bike sheds. The predictability of it makes it all the worse for the target, who becomes terrified of going to the places where he or she expects to be bullied. Some young people miss meals to avoid the lunch queue, or even skip school to avoid bullies.

Terrible impact

Bullying can have terrible and long-lasting effects on someone. In the short term, it makes the target miserable and frightened and may leave him or her with physical injuries. It can damage or destroy someone's **self-esteem**, so the target begins to believe the bullies' view that he or she is weak and worthless.

Young people who are bullied often under-perform at school, as they are unable to concentrate. They may be reluctant to attend school and so start to fall behind. Low self-esteem leads them to expect less of themselves, too. The psychological effects of being bullied can last a lifetime – and can lead the targets to become bullies themselves.

Don't despair

However, if you are being bullied, the situation is not hopeless. Your school can help, and will have established ways of doing so that will not lead to the bully becoming more aggressive towards you. See pages 34–37 for more on what your school will do to help you.

BULLYING IN SCHOOLS

- Rates of bullying vary around the world, but the average is probably 5–15 per cent of children suffering at the hands of bullies.

- In the UK, 15–25 children every year commit suicide because they are being bullied; many more attempt suicide.

- Around one in six children in Australian schools are bullied every week.

- In the USA, a 2007 survey of 12–18-year-olds found that nearly a third of those questioned had been bullied during the school year.

Sometimes, fear of bullies can even stop someone going into school.

2 Am I being bullied?

It can be difficult to admit that you feel you are being bullied. Bullying can cover many different activities – if someone is intentionally making you unhappy again and again, it's bullying.

Just a laugh?

Bullies often say their activity is 'just a laugh' or their target 'can't take a joke'. But it is not a joke or a laugh if it makes someone unhappy. Sometimes, the **aggressor** genuinely means no harm and really does think it's a joke. But if anyone keeps doing something that makes you unhappy after you have asked him or her not to, it is bullying. If it hurts you, or makes you feel miserable, isolated or bad about yourself, it is wrong and you have a right to have it stopped.

Can't I take a joke?

Dear Agony Aunt,
Everyone at my school makes fun of me all the time. They pick on the way I look, the way I speak, my clothes – everything. Even my friends do it. If I ask them to stop, they just say, 'Can't you take a joke?' and go on at me even more. My dad says to take no notice. But I don't think it's funny and it's making me really unhappy.
Sabrina, 14

Dear Sabrina,
If you don't find it funny, then it's not a joke. This kind of persistent picking on someone is bullying, and you have a right to have it taken seriously. Start by talking to a sympathetic adult – perhaps a teacher or another family member. Explain to your dad how unhappy it makes you and he may realize it is more than teasing, but even if he won't take it seriously there are trained people who will. Your school will have a policy for dealing with bullying and this will have guidance on dealing with 'joking' that is not funny.

If your boyfriend or girlfriend bullies you, it's easy to feel there is nowhere to turn. Don't accept someone else's low opinion of you – end the relationship and look for friends who appreciate you.

Making a fuss?

It's not easy to complain that you're being bullied. If the people who are making you unhappy don't believe they are bullying you, they can make you feel bad about your reaction – but you don't have to listen to them. It's your reaction and feelings that count.

Are they really friends?

If your friends or your boyfriend or girlfriend constantly make you the butt of their jokes, laugh at you or use a nickname you don't like, are they really friends? Friends make you feel good, and support you when you are having a bad time. People who make you feel worse and who put you down are not really friends at all.

If the people around you are making you feel bad, it is time to look for new friends and spend time with people who will make you feel better about yourself. Try talking to someone you don't usually speak to, or going to a new club or activity to meet new people. Sometimes, someone you have not thought much about turns out to be just the kind of friend you need.

It's not unusual for someone to be left out or ignored because they are different in some way.

Beyond a joke

It's not just young people who bully others. It's quite common for older people to bully as well, and some of them bully young people and children (see pages 28–31). In particular, older relatives or friends of the family might 'tease' young people and not be able to see when it goes too far. Bullying was often a part of older people's experience of childhood and it was not taken as seriously in the past as it is today. They might say it's harmless fun, or 'It never did me any harm'. But you don't have to put up with it. Ask someone else in your family to have a word with the teaser and tell him or her that it has got beyond a joke.

I wish I could be different

Dear Agony Aunt,
I have ginger hair and although all adults say it's lovely and everyone would want hair like that, I hate it. I'm a bit chubby too. Kids call me 'ginger minger' and 'fat slag' and lots of worse things. I wish I could change my body so that they don't have anything to laugh at, but I can't. If I complain to an adult they just say it's only words and it can't hurt – I should just ignore it. But I think it hurts more than being hit. What can I do?
Laura, 15

Dear Laura,
This is very unpleasant for you, and words often do hurt us much more than physical violence. The adults who say it can't hurt you are wrong. You need to find a sympathetic adult who will help you to deal with this. It's true that ignoring the taunts will make the activity unrewarding for the kids who are bullying you, and they may eventually stop if they don't see you getting upset or cross about it. Ask a teacher to tell you who deals with bullying issues at your school and talk to him or her about what is happening. Your school may also have a counsellor you can talk to.

'Sticks and stones...'

Name-calling and verbal abuse are types of emotional bullying. Emotional bullying is probably the most widespread type of bullying, but many people do not report it unless it gets very bad. Bullies often start by picking on a feature that sets their target apart from other people – it might be a physical characteristic, or an aspect of the target's lifestyle (see pages 24–27). It might start with an unwelcome nickname and can increase to other kinds of verbal abuse, direct insults or taunts, and shouting abuse across a crowded place so that everyone else hears it. Not all verbal abuse is spoken out loud – sometimes a group will pass notes around in class about someone, or write on walls or the target's locker, or leave notes in his or her bag.

FACING BULLIES

Try not to show emotion when bullies say hurtful things – try to remain calm, shrug or walk away, but don't **retaliate**. Even if you are expecting trouble, try not to look like a target.

Jealousy can motivate a bully, so someone who is clever or attractive may end up being bullied.

To hurt their targets, some bullies use weapons – or threaten to use them.

HEALTH WARNING

Although you should not hit out at bullies, you may defend yourself if you are threatened with physical violence. If you respond with more violence, though, you may get into trouble yourself.

Physical bullying

The easiest type of bullying to identify is physical abuse. It covers any kind of unwanted physical contact or violence. At one end of the scale, it can be pushing and shoving someone around, deliberately bashing into them or 'accidentally' knocking them over. Poking, pinching, slapping, scratching and indirect contact such as drenching someone with water or throwing things at them are examples of direct bullying. More serious abuse includes punching, kicking, hitting, strangling, twisting limbs or fingers and Chinese burns. At the top end of the scale are serious injuries caused by cutting, burning, whipping, or tying someone up for a sustained assault. This is extremely unpleasant and dangerous. Physical bullying also includes destroying, stealing or spoiling someone's property.

Hazing

There is a tradition in some schools, clubs and branches of the armed forces of setting tests or trials for new students or members, often involving abuse or violence. For example, new members might have to endure physical punishments or humiliation. This might be called **hazing** or given another name, but it is abusive behaviour and you should report it if you are not happy with what you are asked to do. In some schools, hazing extends to systematic bullying of younger students by older ones.

BULLIES CARRY ON IN CRIME

Research in Scandinavia has found that 60 per cent of people who bully others at school go on to commit other crimes and have a criminal record by the age of 24.

High School Hazing Horror

▷ One girl received a broken ankle

▷ Another girl needed 10 stitches in her head

Hazing, such as this incident reported on American TV and websites, is common in some schools, colleges and the armed forces.

Psychological bullying

Some bullying involves no confrontation between bully and target at all. Psychological bullying often works by isolating and ignoring someone; refusing to speak to the person or include him or her in activities, sports or games. The bullies often put pressure on others to join their campaign of rejection. They may make fun of activities the person likes or the way they live. This is a difficult type of bullying to deal with because it involves a group of people. There may be one or two ringleaders, but they depend on others going along with it. Often, these are

Psychological bullying often involves spreading unpleasant rumours about someone.

Persistent bullying can lead to the target being isolated and suffering alone, unable to confide in friends or family.

people who would never consider themselves bullies and they may not be aware of the degree of harm they are doing. In many cases, it is the target who is forced to change classes or move schools to get away from the problem, though clearly this is unfair.

Rumours and blame

Sometimes, rather than saying things directly to their target, bullies say things to others, spreading **malicious** rumours or blaming the person for things he or she has not done. It can be hard to find the source of rumours to tackle the problem, and it is always difficult to quash a rumour once it has

started. Denying accusations can draw attention to the target and so serves the bullies' purpose.

Making threats

Another type of psychological bullying involves repeatedly threatening someone with violence but never or rarely actually physically hurting them. This is hard for the target to deal with, as the experience can be terrifying but they have no injuries or actual physical harm to report. Bullies may threaten someone with a knife, a gun or fake gun, or with objects which are not usually seen as weapons, such as a baseball bat, hockey stick, rocks, a heavy bag or a cigarette lighter.

FAQ

3 What is cyber-bullying?

Nearly all young people use technology such as computers and mobile phones to keep in touch with friends. These provide another means for bullies to attack their targets. This 'cyber-bullying' can be effective and may seem difficult to tackle.

HEALTH WARNING

Be careful who you give your phone number to. If you start to get abusive calls or texts, you can easily change your number; then you can start again, giving your number only to people you trust.

Receiving unpleasant text messages can be extremely distressing and even frightening.

What can I do about abusive text messages?

Dear Agony Aunt,
Someone I thought was my friend has starting sending me horrible text messages because I'm going out with a boy she likes. She calls me a slag, and says she'll slash my face so I'm ugly and he won't like me. Now, as soon as I get a text from her, I delete it without reading it, but I'm still scared.
Carlie, 15

Dear Carlie,
Firstly, don't respond to her texts – she will just send more. You or your boyfriend must tell this girl to stop sending you these messages. If that does not stop her, you'll need to take it further. Deleting the messages means that you have no record of the abuse. Keep messages from her, but you don't need to read them immediately. Do you have a sibling or friend who would read them with you or for you? Contact your phone network – they might be able to have her phone account suspended. (They will be able to find her network.) Sending threatening messages is a criminal offence. You can contact the police as long as you have kept the messages she has sent to you as evidence.

Phone bullies

Bullying by phone may take the form of nuisance, abusive or silent phone calls, or abusive or threatening text messages. Bullies might repeatedly phone someone in the night to disrupt his or her sleep, or send frightening or abusive text messages. Sending sexually explicit text messages, or distressing sexual picture messages, is sometimes called 'sexting'.

Anonymous abuse

It's easy for someone to send text messages anonymously, and then you won't know who is bullying you. If this happens, contact your phone network with a note of the times and dates you received the messages, and ask them to trace and block the phone that has been used to send the texts.

'By virtue of technology the bully not only follows you home but is invited into your house ... into your child's bedroom, the one place that they should be safe.'

Susan McLean, Cyber-safety Advisor, Victoria, Australia

The person who films or photographs an incident of 'happy slapping' is as guilty as the person who kicks or punches the target.

CHAT

An instant messaging or chat service such as MSN or Facebook chat makes it easy for a bully to be directly abusive to someone. If you are the subject of an attack like this, it is easy to close the chat session and block the bully from contacting you again. Don't get involved in an exchange of abuse in a chat session – just end the session.

Happy slapping

Happy slapping combines technology with physical bullying in a particularly distressing way. One bully uses a mobile phone to film others abusing or assaulting the target. The bully then shares the video online or by showing it to others. For the target of a happy-slapping assault, the event is doubly traumatic, as the physical injury and fear are followed by public humiliation.

Bullying by computer

Computers make it very easy for bullies to extend their reach into the target's wider social group and the personal space of his or her home. Bullying by computer often takes place on social networking sites, in instant messaging sessions and in online games. It can also involve uploading and sharing videos or photos of someone, perhaps changed to make them look strange or ugly. Items posted on the Internet are almost impossible to get rid of, as they are so easily copied from place to place. This makes online bullying particularly distressing.

As in real-world bullying, cyber-bullying may involve isolating someone, perhaps blocking them from an online game, or ignoring them in a chat session.

Bullied online

Nearly three in four American teenagers say they were bullied online at least once during a 12-month period in 2004–5; 85 per cent of those had also been bullied at school. Only ten per cent of those bullied reported it to a parent or other adult; a third said they didn't report the abuse in case parents restricted their access to the Internet.

HEALTH WARNING

If you are going to use a **forum** or chat site, choose one **moderated** by human **moderators**, not just monitored by software. Software moderation often lets through abusive posts if the spelling of unacceptable words is non-standard. Check the information the site provides about how it keeps you safe. There should be details there about whether the site is moderated and what to do if you are badly treated by someone.

Computers offer bullies a way of attacking someone in his or her own home.

Antisocial networking

Dear Agony Aunt,
Someone at school keeps posting untrue things about me on the social networking site we all use. They have put up photos of me, changed to make me look stupid, and started a group called 'Charise sucks'. What can I do? I can't tell my mum – she'll stop me using the computer.
Charise, 15

Dear Charise,
This is very upsetting for you. If someone writes comments on your own page, you can delete them, but you can't delete messages and photos they may post on another page. In either case, you need to find the link on the networking site to report abuse. The administrators will take down the abusive posts and warn the bullies not to do it. The bullies' accounts will be suspended if they carry on. You can do the same if someone posts photos or videos of you on a file-sharing site such as Flickr or YouTube.

IT HAPPENED TO ME

Leanne, who used to be my friend, starting posting horrible things on my Bebo page. I blocked her, but she put them on her own page, and then started a group that was called 'Abigail is a lesbian hooker' and invited everyone I knew to join. Eventually, the head at my school wrote to Leanne's mum, who blocked Leanne from using the computer.

Abigail, 13

KILLED BY FACEBOOK

British teenager Holly Grogan, 15, jumped from a bridge onto a busy road and was killed by traffic after suffering prolonged bullying on Facebook. Holly had been bullied at school, and changed schools once to escape bullies. Cyber-bullying is increasingly common and has been linked with several teen suicides.

Cyber-bullying is easy for cowards

It is much easier to bully someone online than in person. The lack of physical confrontation means the bully cannot see the response of the target. People who might stop short of upsetting someone they can see may take part in a cyber-bullying campaign without really thinking about it. Some cyber-bullying is even carried out anonymously, though most targets know their bullies.

Avoid hacker bullies

Keep your passwords secure and change them from time to time. This will avoid anyone hacking into your account on a game or social networking site and vandalizing it. Always log out when you have finished using the computer, so that no one else can use your account.

Print copies of abusive messages sent to you on the computer and take them to your school when you complain about bullying. It doesn't matter that the cyber-bullying happened outside school – the school can still help.

Keeping evidence

As with any kind of bullying, evidence of what has happened is very useful when you are seeking help. Keep abusive text messages, print copies of bullying emails, chat sessions and comments on social networking sites. All these will help you to demonstrate what has been going on, and can be used in any **mediation** sessions or even a prosecution.

Getting help

The Internet can be a valuable source of help if you are being bullied or cyber-bullied. There are many online support groups offering advice, **helpline** information and a chance to share experiences with other people in a similar position (see page 45).

ONLINE SUPPORT

There are bullying support groups online, including some on social networking sites such as Facebook. Anti-bullying and support groups can offer advice and a sympathetic ear. You can often join a group without having it show on your profile, so others won't see you are using it. If you are worried, you can set up a separate account or profile and use that to access the support you want.

4 Why are they bullying me?

Anyone can be a target for bullies. If you are being bullied, it is not your fault and it does not say anything bad about you. For example, some very successful and famous people were bullied when they were young, often because of the talents that led to their later success.

Bullies might exclude someone from group activities on account of his or her race or religious beliefs.

It's easier for bullies to pick on someone physically weaker or smaller, or someone who is alone.

'Often the teasing and bullying comes from children who know they aren't going to be the ones winning things. Disaffected pupils have low self-esteem and try to bring down the other children to their level.'

Fran Baker, Assistant Head, Edenham High School, Croydon, UK

What makes you different?

Often, bullies pick on someone who is different in some way. It could be an aspect of physical appearance, such as being bigger or smaller than other people, having ginger hair, wearing glasses, having a physical disability or obvious feature such as acne or a scar. Or it may be a different attribute, even something that you would expect people to be impressed by, such as being very good at sport, or very clever, or having modelling or acting contracts. It can be something to do with your lifestyle, religion, ethnic background, social class or **sexual orientation**.

Picking on vulnerable people

Bullies target people they think are vulnerable. They may be physically vulnerable, or vulnerable in other ways. A young person who has just moved to a new area or school may not have friends to back him or her up against the bullies, for instance. Someone who has been in trouble in the past may not be able to hit back in case they are accused of starting a fight.

IT HAPPENED TO ME

A group of kids at school hate me because I'm clever and work hard. They call me a boff and on the way home they grab my bag and throw my books out. Last month, one of them took my bag and hit me hard with it in the stomach. I keep a lower profile now. I still work hard, but also make myself more obvious in sport and drama so they think of me differently.

Mustafa, 14

MENTAL DISABILITY AND BULLYING

A survey by the mental health organization Mencap in 2007 found that 82 per cent of children with a learning disability are bullied and 79 per cent are scared to go out because they are afraid of bullies.

Bullied for being 'gay'

Dear Agony Aunt,
Some boys at my school have started to call me 'gay boy'. They leave obscene notes and pictures in my locker, they have put links to gay pornography on my Facebook page, which I have to keep deleting, and they have threatened to do horrible things to me. I can't tell my parents because they are very anti-gay.
Sid, 16

Dear Sid,
Bullying someone because of his or her sexuality is very common, sadly. Whether or not you are gay, it is wrong for bullies to target your sexuality. If you don't feel you can talk to your parents about it, talk to someone at your school. Please don't be embarrassed. This type of bullying can destroy your confidence in yourself and your personal style if it is not tackled. It might help to talk to someone about your sexuality if you need reassurance.

ANTI-GAY BULLIES

Nearly two-thirds of homosexual pupils in Britain's schools have suffered homophobic bullying according to a survey in 2007.

Of those, 41 per cent had been physically attacked and 17 per cent had received death threats.

Being bullied for your sexual orientation – or what people believe your sexual orientation to be – is surprisingly common.

Public events that promote tolerance, such as this rally against homophobia, help to reduce bullying that results from ignorance of different lifestyles.

Not your fault

It is never your fault if you are bullied. Nothing you have done makes you 'deserve' to be bullied. However, the bullies will probably try to make you feel it is your fault and that it 'serves you right'.

If you are bullied for your race, religion or sexuality, there may be anti-discrimination laws that will protect you and that teachers or parents can use to help stop the bullying. The police may get involved if the bullying is very serious or is **discriminatory** in this way.

Why be a bully at all?

It's hard to see what motivates someone to bully others. Often, people bully because they can get away with it. They enjoy the sense of control, and if the target responds by being frightened this makes the bully feel more powerful. Some people who become bullies have been bullied or abused themselves, or have seen lots of violence at home. Some have little self-esteem and bullying makes them 'feel big'. At the other end of the spectrum, some bullies are confident show-offs who feel superior to others and do it to flaunt their power.

FAQ

5 What if the bully is an adult?

Although most young people who are bullied suffer at the hands of people their own age, it is sometimes an adult who bullies a young person. This can be difficult to combat, as other adults may be reluctant to believe that this happens.

Adult bullies

Not all bullies grow out of their unpleasant behaviour. Some people continue to bully and abuse others into adulthood. Those who were

My teacher bullies me

Dear Agony Aunt,
My geography teacher picks on me to answer difficult questions, then ridicules my answers. When my friend and I get the same answers, she gets a better mark than I do. I get detention for things other people get away with. He says in front of other people that I'm lazy and stupid. What can I do? No one will believe me if I complain and I'm scared of getting into trouble if I do.
Biragaba, 14

Dear Biragaba,
It can be difficult to get people to take your accusations seriously, but they will if you can present a clear case. Keep a diary of everything insulting your teacher says to you, noting the circumstances and date, and when you get an unfair mark. You could challenge your teacher calmly and ask why you are being treated like this, but you may prefer to go to a senior member of staff. Will other students back up your claims? If so, ask them to help. Your teacher is acting unprofessionally and the school should have a system to deal with his bullying.

Teachers and other people in positions of power and responsibility sometimes bully those they should be looking after.

bullied as children may grow up to become adult bullies. Their targets may be other adults, children or young people.

Adults who bully young people

Adults can bully young people if they are in a position of authority and can deal with them one-to-one, often with no other adults present. This could mean family members, teachers, religious leaders, leaders of social groups or activities, sports leaders and coaches, a babysitter or someone else employed to look after young people.

IT HAPPENED TO ME

This sounds really stupid but my uncle Terry tickles my little brother until he wets himself. He used to do it to me, too, when I was younger. My uncle thinks it's funny. It might have been funny once, but for a 10-year-old it's the most humiliating thing in the world. Adrian can't bear to go anywhere near him. I know now I should have complained when it happened to me, but next time we see him I'm going to speak out for Adrian because I feel so bad about it.

Sebastian, 13

IT HAPPENED TO ME

My hockey coach used to bully me and another kid. He made us run round and round the field when other kids didn't have to. When I had an asthma attack, he still made me run. He used to yell at me and say I was useless. I hated going to hockey. When we went on a tournament, he made me eat the food I was served at lunch, even though I hate it. It made me sick, and then he shouted at me for that. Eventually I persuaded my dad the coach was bullying me and I didn't have to go any more.

Zach, 14

What adult bullies do

Adult bullies may not physically hurt young people, but harm them in other ways. They may deliberately tell someone off for something that person hasn't done, or insult and belittle him or her, often in front of other people so that it is humiliating. They might treat someone unfairly or unkindly, such as not letting him or her go to the toilet, or spoiling the person's food. Bullying can also involve sexual harassment and unwelcome physical contact.

Will anyone take me seriously?

It can be difficult to persuade someone to take you seriously if you complain that you are being bullied by an adult – many people prefer to believe the adult. Keep a log of what has happened to you, and

Bullying in sports is not unusual – the competitive atmosphere and high tension can lead to inappropriate behaviour.

Bullying by a family member can be very hard to live with, as it seems there is nowhere to turn. School can be a refuge and a source of support.

ask for support from anyone who has witnessed the bullying. Keep calm when you complain to a parent or teacher about adult bullying and explain patiently that you need them to take you seriously and investigate. The more reasonable and mature you are, the more likely they are to take you seriously immediately.

Don't over-react!

It is not bullying if your parents make you eat the same food as other people instead of cooking what you like, if you are forced to do sports at school, or made to practise a musical instrument. It is not bullying if your parents keep you off the computer or confiscate your phone when you disobey them.

FAQ

6 How can I make it stop?

Someone who is being bullied is usually feeling frightened and fragile, so it can seem like an impossible task to tackle the bully and stop his or her behaviour. It is not impossible, though – there are plenty of people ready to help.

Will they stop?

Some people who are bullied hope that eventually the bullies will get bored and stop, but that rarely happens. If no one intervenes, bullying can go on for months or even years.

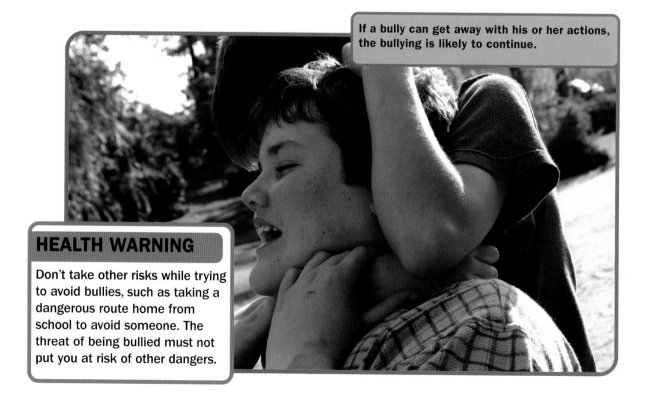

If a bully can get away with his or her actions, the bullying is likely to continue.

HEALTH WARNING

Don't take other risks while trying to avoid bullies, such as taking a dangerous route home from school to avoid someone. The threat of being bullied must not put you at risk of other dangers.

The bullies will hurt me more

Dear Agony Aunt,
I'm being bullied by two girls at school. When I threatened to tell, they laughed and said no one would believe me. They're probably right – they're popular and I'm not. They said if I even tried, they would beat my sister. If it was just me, I might risk it – but I'm really scared of them doing something to my sister, who's only 11. What can I do?
Caitlin, 13

Dear Caitlin,
*If the bullies can scare you into keeping quiet they can get on with bullying you, can't they? As the bullies are based at your school, you can call on the **anti-bullying policy** of the school to protect you both. Tell your parents, and also ask a teacher or school counsellor who you should report bullying to at school. You can explain everything that has happened and ask for protection before you give the names of the bullies, if you like. Perhaps your sister could be picked up from school for a while, or share a lift or walk home with someone else. Or maybe she could have a 'bully buddy' – this is an older student or a member of staff who will look after her while this is sorted out. But don't let the bullies get away with it – they won't stop unless you make them stop.*

BE ASSERTIVE!

Assertiveness training can help you to stand up to bullies, or learning some self-defence or a sport such as karate may help you to feel better. You don't have to use your new skill to hit out – but knowing you can look after yourself will make you feel more confident and improve your self-esteem.

Joining a club or group also means you will meet new people and perhaps make new friends. It can help you build up a part of your life that is quite separate from the bullying and that in turn will help you to feel better and enjoy life again.

Sharing your problem by talking about the bullying with someone who will be sympathetic is a good first step.

Telling someone

Bullies rely on the isolation of their target, so the first step in combatting bullying is to talk to someone to make sure you are not isolated. If you can, tell a trusted adult – a member of your family, a teacher, a religious leader, the parent of a friend, or an adult friend. If you are too scared to tell an adult, or don't know who to trust, tell a close friend or an older brother or sister as a first step. He or she might be able to help you choose an adult to confide in or may be able to help you sort out the problem.

Help at school

If you are bullied at school, look at what your school does to help you report bullying. There may be a bullying box where you can report bullying (of yourself or of someone else), and perhaps a **bullying court** where pupils can deal with bullying without involving staff. You may be able to ask for a buddy to be with you at times when you are vulnerable, such as at break or on the way home. There may be a 'safe room' you can go to if you feel threatened. Your school should have an anti-bullying policy, which sets out how it will deal with bullying. You can ask to see this and then you will know what to expect.

Work out what to say

Take a little time to work out what you are going to say; you will feel more confident if it is clear in your mind. Make sure you have some evidence. You may not have injuries to show, but perhaps you have saved abusive text messages, or you have some things that have been spoiled, or a record of dates and times when you have been bullied. You can still report the problem even if you are not willing to say who the bullies are (or if you don't know who they are).

HELPLINES

If you are feeling desperate and there is no one to speak to immediately, you can contact a helpline (see page 45). Helplines are staffed by people trained to deal with your problems. They will listen if you want to talk, they can give advice if you want it and they can tell you where to go for more help. They will not pass on anything you say unless you tell them to. The call is free, and you can call at any time, day or night.

Calling a helpline can be very reassuring when you are feeling low, and the operators can give you advice about how to get help.

Talking to a teacher, counsellor or bullying specialist at school is a way to begin resolving a problem with bullies.

What your school will do

Your school will probably draw up a plan for dealing with your problem. They may move the bully to a different class to reduce his or her contact with you. You should insist that it is not you that is moved, unless you want to move – you have done nothing wrong. They might improve supervision in areas where bullying takes place, such as toilets, corridors and playgrounds. The school may appoint a buddy or mentor to help keep an eye on you and give you someone to talk to about the problem. Peer counselling might be possible. This gives you the chance to talk to another young person, perhaps someone who has already dealt with bullying successfully. You may be invited to a counselling session or perhaps a mediation session with the bully or bullies. This can be challenging, but it is important to consider going to a session like this, as it can really help. Often, this is the first time bullies really understand the impact their behaviour has. You could also ask to have a friend or the school counsellor with you for support.

Persistent bullying

If bullying is persistent and serious, the school may have to do more than just talk to the bullies. The bullies may face a formal punishment such as suspension or even exclusion. Their parents may be involved if it is necessary to stop behaviour outside school, such as cyber-bullying. If the situation is very serious, the police may become involved. In some cases, you may be assigned a social worker or other support worker to help you.

Examining the school's anti-bullying policy will show you what help you can expect from your school.

HEALTH WARNING

Some adults may be reluctant to believe you are being bullied because they don't want to have to deal with it, or they don't want to believe something bad about the other person. This is especially true if that person is popular, polite to adults or in a position of responsibility, such as a teacher or prefect. They might try to make light of it, or tell you not to be a 'wimp'. If you get this response, ask a different person to help you. Stay calm, but insistent – you have a right to help.

IT TAKES TWO (AT LEAST)

Any bullying situation involves at least two people – the target and the bully or bullies. Stopping the bullying is important for both parties. If you are being bullied, don't feel bad about getting a bully into trouble, even if it is someone you may once have considered your friend. Stopping bullying will be good for them, too, in the long run.

FAQ

7 Am I a bully?

Bullies aren't always other people. It's easy to engage in bullying behaviour without really thinking about it or recognizing it. Many people are simultaneously bullies, targets and **bystanders** who let bullying happen.

Mean actions may look like a bit of fun if you are being thoughtless – but you are on the bullies' side if you enjoy watching someone being ridiculed or hurt.

Bully or target?

A study in Colorado, USA, found that 80 per cent of school students questioned had taken part in some form of bullying behaviour in the previous 30 days. Many had also been the target of bullying. Being bullied makes the target more likely to bully others, either immediately or later. Some experts think it is not helpful to label a young person as either a bully or a target of bullying, but to treat bullying behaviour. It is then easier for people who feel they have behaved in a bullying way to seek to change.

Thoughtless bullying and bystanders

It's easy to behave in a bullying way without realizing you are doing it or meaning anyone any harm. There might be times when you have joined in with excluding someone or laughing at him or her, maybe even thinking it a joke, but perhaps upsetting that person. It's easy to be a bystander, too – someone who observes bullying behaviour but does not speak out against it or try to stop it.

HEALTH WARNING

It takes courage to speak out against bullying going on around you, but it is an admirable thing to do. However, do not put yourself in danger while trying to stop bullying. It is often better to go to an adult for help than to intervene in a violent situation.

'It looks like bullying is a **continuum** of behaviours. Rather than labelling a kid a bully, a non-bully or a victim, it seems that many of the students engage in bullying behaviour, although most reported low to moderate levels of that behaviour.'

Dr Dorothy Espelage, University of Illinois at Urbana-Champaign, USA

WHAT WOULD MAKE ME A BULLY?

If you have done any of the following things, you have acted in a bullying way, even if unwittingly:

- Joined in when others have refused to speak to someone or not invited that person to take part in group activities.
- Laughed at or made hurtful remarks about someone's appearance, accent, background or clothes.
- Spoiled someone's schoolwork, possessions or food 'as a joke'.
- Passed on gossip, messages, photos or videos of someone, online or in the real world, knowing that the person would not like it.

As a bystander, not speaking out against bullying makes you partly responsible.

WHY MIGHT YOU DO IT?

These are some of the reasons people give for engaging in bullying behaviour. Maybe you can recognize something that relates to you:

- 'Everyone else is doing it and I just joined in.'
- 'I was scared if I didn't join in, I'd be the next target.'
- 'It's a laugh.'
- '(S)he deserves it.'
- 'I'm bullied – I need to take it out on someone else.'

None of these is ever a valid reason, and no one ever deserves to be bullied.

HEALTH WARNING

Bullying behaviour can quickly escalate. This can have repercussions for the bully as well as the target. The bully may be excluded from school, missing important exams, or may get into trouble with the police. A criminal record threatens the ability to travel to some countries and will close many career paths forever.

If you see one of your friends bullying, try to intervene immediately. It takes courage, but it's the most effective thing to do.

Facing up to it

Many people are bullies at some time in their lives. Most would rather deny it, or not think about it. Some people bully others to feel big, and because they enjoy the feeling of power and control. But bullying is cowardly: it is far braver to face what you have been doing and seek help to change.

Owning up

Find out about bullying support at your school – there should be measures to help bullies as well as their targets. You may be able to go to counselling sessions, for example, or take an **anger management course**. You might be asked to have a face-to-face meeting with someone who has been bullied and hear how bullying affected him or her. This can be hard to do, but you will gain understanding and insight. If you can once put yourself in the target's shoes, you may feel very differently about your behaviour.

I know it's happening...

Dear Agony Aunt,
My friend Daniel bullies another boy on the school bus. I know this kid is really frightened and unhappy, but Daniel just thinks it's a laugh. When I said he shouldn't do it, he just said I was being soft.
Ahmed, 14

Dear Ahmed,
You're right to be concerned. If the boy is unhappy, then Daniel's behaviour is not 'a laugh' and must be stopped. Speak to him about it again – maybe in a loud voice on the bus. This would tell the boy where you stand – and it may give others the courage to speak out too. You could also move to sit next to the boy. If Daniel still won't back off, tell an adult – perhaps a parent or teacher. This will be hard, because Daniel is your friend. But in the long run it will help him, too – if he continues to be a bully, he will lose friends and possibly get into serious trouble. You can tell in confidence; the school will not tell Daniel you spoke out if you don't want them to. But if you let it continue, you are contributing to the boy's unhappiness.

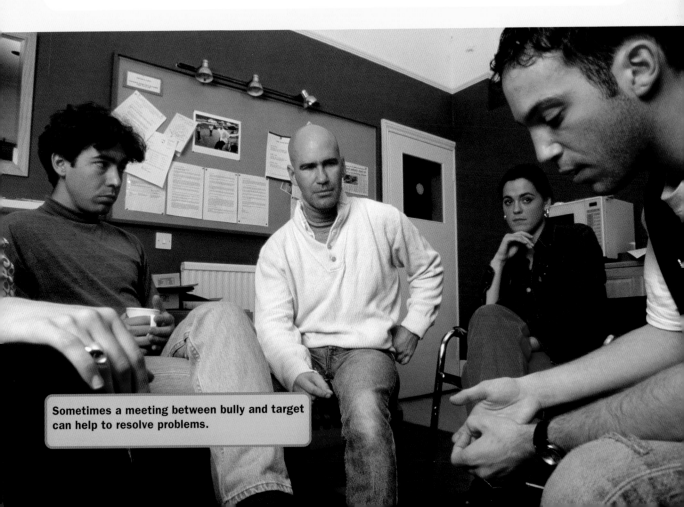

Sometimes a meeting between bully and target can help to resolve problems.

FAQ

8 Tackling bullying

For each individual confronting bullying, the problem is immediate and personal, and he or she needs immediate, personal solutions. But bullying needs to be tackled on a larger scale, too.

Children who are bullied sometimes grow up to be bullies themselves – it's important to sort out bullying for everyone concerned.

A climate of bullying

Much advice about dealing with bullying puts the responsibility for solving the problem onto the target. Bullying is not just a problem for the person being bullied, but for all of us – bullies, targets, bystanders, schools and the rest of society. There are still many people who belittle the issue of bullying. This allows it to go unchallenged and even to be socially acceptable in some circles.

Education

The key to real and lasting change is education. Not only young people in schools, but adults in the community and the workplace must be informed about bullying – how to recognize it, how to combat it and how damaging it is for the targets of bullying. This will not happen overnight, but the more often people speak out against bullying, the more quickly it will happen.

'There's a real value system around [bullying] that basically teaches kids that it's not just okay – it's more than okay. Social acceptability of bullying is a consequence of many complex things that teach them that being mean is not only acceptable, but good.'

Howard Spivak, Professor of Paediatrics and Community Health, Tufts University, Massachusetts, USA

Having a happy, active life can raise your self-esteem, and having good self-esteem helps you overcome problems.

HELP YOURSELF FEEL BETTER

Being bullied causes low self-esteem, and that can lead to physical and psychological health problems. Never accept the bully's low estimation of your worth. Make time to do things you like and are good at, spend time with people you like and who value you, and eat and sleep properly – if you get run down, you will find it harder to cope. Sport or exercise is good, as exercise makes the body release **hormones** that make you feel good.

Glossary

aggressor a person who is aggressive towards another, or starts trouble

anger management course a course that teaches people how to deal with anger in a healthy way, without getting violent, aggressive or depressed

anti-bullying policy a set of measures a school or other organization puts in place to give a structure in which it can challenge bullying and sort out bullying problems

bullying court a meeting between a person who has been bullied, supported by friends, and the bully, to sort out the bullying

bystander a person who does not take part in an activity, but watches or does not act to stop it

continuum a continuous set or range

cyber-bullying bullying someone using communications technology such as a phone or computer

discriminatory describes the singling out of people for unfair treatment on account of a feature such as age, gender, ethnic origins or religion

forum a space for talk or discussion

harass to repeatedly torment someone on purpose

hazing organized bullying that takes place in a school, club or the armed forces

helpline a telephone line which provides support for a particular type of problem

hormone a chemical produced by the body and acting as a chemical 'messenger', controlling other aspects of the body's chemical activity

humiliation shaming someone in front of others to make him or her feel bad

intervene to interfere to stop trouble

intimidate to frighten someone by means of a threat

malicious deliberately harmful or spiteful

mediation helping people to talk through their issues and resolve problems by providing a third person who will sit in on their discussion, guide it in helpful directions and suggest solutions and compromises

moderate to look after a forum or chat site to make sure abuse does not take place

moderator someone who keeps an eye on what happens in a web chat room to make sure no one abuses anyone or uses bad language

psychological relating to the mind or mental state

retaliate to take action to get back at someone when they do something unpleasant or aggressive

self-esteem a person's belief in his or her own worth

sexual orientation sexual preference; whether someone is attracted to members of the same or opposite sex

vulnerable used to describe a situation in which someone is more likely to be hurt or harmed

Further information

WEBSITES

www.cyh.com/HealthTopics/HealthTopicDetails.aspx?p=243&np=295&id=2197
Useful information on recognizing and dealing with bullying, whether you are the target or the bully.

www.bullying.co.uk/
News, issues and advice relating to bullying – the website also has connections on Twitter, Facebook and Flickr.

www.antibullying.net/youngpeople.htm
Advice and personal stories from young people aged 11+.

www.nspcc.org.uk/under18/bullying/bullying_wda38474.html
Advice for under-18s on identifying and tackling bullying and child abuse.

www.childline.org.uk/Explore/Bullying/Pages/Bullying.aspx
Useful questions and answers and a video testament from the target of bullies.

HELPLINES

NSPCC Child Protection Helpline: 0808 800 5000 or help@nspcc.org.uk

ChildLine: 0800 1111 or online chat at
http://www.childline.org.uk/Talk/Chat/Pages/OnlineChat.aspx

Samaritans: 08457 909090 or jo@samaritans.org

BOOKS

Jenny Alexander, *Bullies, Bigmouths and So-called Friends*, Hodder Children's Books, 2006

Jane Bingham, *Let's Talk About Bullying*, Wayland, 2008

Deborah Chancellor, *Bullying (Your Call)*, Franklin Watts, 2009

John Mattern, *Bullying (The Real Deal)*, Heinemann, 2009

Rosemary Stones, *Don't Pick on Me: How to Handle Bullying*, Piccadilly Press, 2005

Index